The Resident Manager's Handbook

The Resident Manager's Handbook

Pierre Mouchette

The Resident Manager's Handbook

ISBN 13: 978-1537526805
ISBN 10: 1537526804
Printed in the United States

This publication is designed to provide accurate and authoritative information with regard to the subject matter covered. It is sold with the understanding that the publisher is not engaged in rendering legal, accounting, or other professional advice. If legal advice or other expert assistance is required, the services of a competent professional person should be sought (from a *Declaration of Principles* jointly adopted by a Committee of the American Bar Association and a Committee of Publishers and Associations).

Library of Congress Control Number: 2016914969
CreateSpace Independent Publishing Platform, North Charleston, SC

This book is dedicated to the most important people in my life:
Tomasa, Yolanda, Nona,
Albert, Pierre, Paul, and Jean-Pierre,
wife and children respectively.

I would also like to express a special thank-you to
Tomasa, my wife,
for her contribution in helping to edit the manuscript.
She spent many evenings and weekends
reading every word of each and every page.
I appreciate her observations,
thoughts, and, above all, patience and time.

Contents

The Resident Manager's Handbook

PREFACE

The Resident Manager's Handbook will provide the reader with a list of duties to be performed by the resident manager and the members of his or her team. Of utmost importance is the resident manager's ability to monitor the work of other team members for "make-ready services." Also included is a list of "resident-responsible repairs" so the resident manager will not be overwhelmed by the "I want...I want" resident.

This manual may contain general legal and accounting principles and is not meant to be a substitute for consulting an attorney and an accountant. It is to be used as a guide for obtaining the indicated use.

The book is written in an easy-to-read format for instant implementation.

Pierre Mouchette, author

SECTION 1   JOB RESPONSIBILITIES

1.0   Title

The title of the position is resident manager. Although the position carries a title, the resident manager is an independent contractor and not an employee. The relationship between the independent contractor and the property owner is created by a written contract signed by both parties, which empowers the resident manager to act on behalf of the property owner in a custodial capacity.

1.1   Job Description

The resident manager is vested with the primary responsibility for all aspects of the day-to-day operation of the apartment community. This position requires strong administrative and public relations skills and competence in written and verbal communications. The resident manager must be organized, motivated, and detail oriented.

The primary function of the resident manager is to

- maintain an on-site presence of management;

- maximize the asset manager's income in every possible way;

- minimize expenses whenever possible;

- deal with any situations at hand, whether they be tenant relations or problems; and

- protect the owner's investment.

The resident manager should read often and understand this handbook, the Fair Housing Act, and the state's landlord tenant laws.

The resident manager is hired and directed by the asset manager, who in turn is one of the owners of the investment property. Good communication between the resident manager and the asset manager is crucial in maintaining the proper operation of the apartment community.

The contract period for the resident manager is to be no longer than one year, with extensions of contract as required. The contract can be terminated for cause by either party with thirty days' notice.

The resident manager must at all times

- maintain a professional, courteous, knowledgeable, and helpful attitude with past, present, and potential residents and convey this attitude to all **team members**; and

- be honest, respectful, and truthful with residents and team members.

The types of **residential buildings** that the **resident manager** contracts for are:

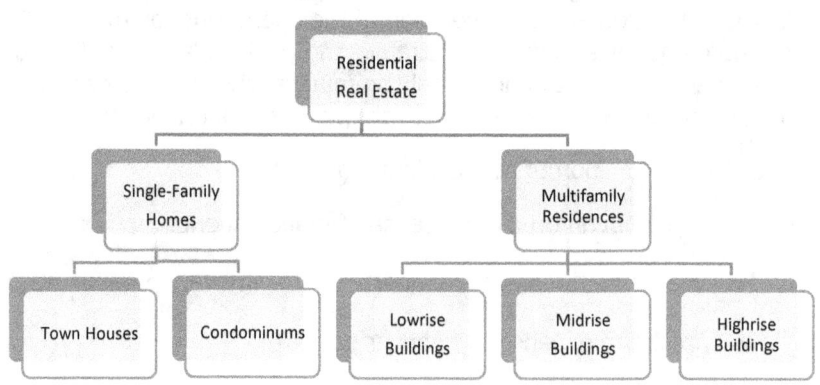

1.2   Job Duties

Property management is an exciting and challenging occupation. The resident manager wears many different hats and must be able to handle multiple tasks. The property manager must live on site and oversee the entire operation of the apartment community. The position is typically a "team" effort so that all aspects of managing the apartment community (administration, tenant relation, maintenance, and grounds keeping) can be handled. Of utmost importance is the availability of at least one of the team members during office hours to answer telephone calls and provide tours to prospective tenants. The resident manager must remember at all times that he or she is a representative of the owner and that he or she should handle all situations in the most ethical, professional manner possible. The resident manager is to provide all work duties as described herein.

Administrative

- Show apartments, provide applications, and collect application fees. All paperwork to be submitted to the asset manager within twenty-four hours;

- Read and understand all training materials and updates forwarded to him or her by the asset manager;

- Communicate effectively with the residents in addressing problems and keeping them up to date on resident issues;

- Complete reports as required;

- Prepare the apartments for new tenant occupancy;

- Facilitate team members;

- Maintain responsibility for the inventory of tools, supplies, furniture, etc.; and

- Be fully responsible for the master keys.

Operations

- Conduct morning inspections in the building(s) and throughout the grounds;

- Ensure that a monthly detailed cleaning checklist is completed each month;

- Keep the grounds and parking lot free of litter and debris; and

- Inspect the boiler rooms and mechanical room daily.

Grounds Keeping

- Ensure that the lawn is cut regularly and that the weeds around the buildings, curbs, sidewalks, trees, and fences are trimmed regularly to the height of the lawn.

- Maintain the shrubs so that they look properly trimmed;

- Sweep the sidewalks regularly; and

- Remove snow from all entrance areas, sidewalks, and steps by 8:00 a.m. each morning and on an as-needed basis as the day progresses.

- Make prompt arrangements for the removal of snow from the parking lot.

General Maintenance and Upkeep of the Property

The appearance of the property is important. Prospective residents form their initial impressions of the premises based on what they see as they approach the building.

- Pick up trash on the grounds and in the building interior and monitor for cleanliness;

- Clean the hallways, stairs, and common areas;

- Troubleshoot maintenance problems, coordinate maintenance operations, and ensure quality repairs;

- Coordinate snow shoveling;

- Coordinate landscaping; and

- And other duties as directed by the asset manager.

Maintenance

- Provide first-line maintenance, making sure any deficiencies are corrected as soon as possible.

- Promptly write up service requests for routine and low-maintenance repairs.

- Work with the assigned maintenance technician to ensure timely repairs.

- Monitor subcontractors and ensure prompt and proper completion of repairs.

- Check all indoor and outdoor lighting daily.

Resident Manager Maintenance Plan

To keep the property in the best possible shape, the resident manager should prepare a maintenance plan and submit it to the asset manager.

Planned Works and Improvements

Major work will be programmed at least three months in advance, and the frequency of such works will be determined according to the expected life of key building components.

To respond to a resident's needs:

- The resident manager is responsible for responding to a resident's needs.

- Follow up immediately on a resident's complaints and phone calls regarding suspicious activities or security problems.

- Be a good and fair arbitrator when necessary.

- Assist residents with problems and requests to the best of your ability and to the limits of your authority.

- Make any necessary repairs or improvements.

To communicate and meet with the asset manager.

- The resident manager should call the asset manager to report any problems that he or she cannot handle.

The resident manager will not negotiate rent with prospective residents. (State laws require a real estate license to negotiate rents.)

1.3   Policy

Update and maintain your resident manager handbook with information as received from the asset manager.

Use the forms provided to you by the asset manager. You may not alter any form. Discuss your recommendations for revisions or additional forms with the asset manager.

1.4   Rentals

Prepare apartments to show to prospective residents within two days after a previous resident has moved out.

Show readied apartments and the community to prospective residents. Always be consistent with your presentation.

If a prospect is interested, fill out all required documents and photocopy driver's licenses, Social Security cards, and pay stubs as required.

Forward information (via fax) to the asset manager for (resident) approval.

If an applicant is rejected by the asset manager, an explanation letter will be sent out by the asset manager. The resident manager is not to get involved in this!

If an applicant is a valid candidate for tenancy, the appropriate documents will be available via e-mail for your download. Call the applicant using positive telephone technique. Invite him or her to the property to

- sign lease agreement;

- take digital photographs of all residents; and

- make copies of all documents not previously obtained or made.

Always refer prospective residents to other communities owned by the asset manager if you are unable to satisfy their housing needs. Refer to a weekly faxed availability list, and call that apartment's resident manager to verify if the apartment is still available.

Know your property! Know your competition and the area market by referring to the Threats, Opportunities, Weaknesses, and Strengths (TOWS) chart in your resident manager package. Provide an updated copy at end of month to the asset manager.

Keep all appropriate information on the property in its appropriate file.

Maintain your traffic sheets and phone logs. Provide a copy at the end of the month to the asset manager.

Before the resident moves in, verify that **all** paperwork is complete and correct and that the proper rent and security have been paid. Verify that the electricity is on. Be sure the locks have been changed and that the welcome basket is in the apartment. Coordinate work and inspect and digitally photograph each apartment before move in to ensure it is ready for occupancy. Escort the new resident into the apartment and record all move-in conditions on the standard move-in form. Make a copy of the move-in report and make requested repairs as soon as possible. Have the resident initial and date each item corrected.

At move out, complete all inspections, photographs, and paperwork promptly and thoroughly. Charge residents for damages beyond normal wear and tear. Protect the asset manager's interest.

Remind residents of their intent to renew or vacate at least three months prior to the expiration of the lease. Follow up until the notification deadline.

1.5   Rents

Handle late rents and bad checks promptly, according to proper procedure.

Waive late fees only one time in the course of the lease period. Late fees may be waived only for a good resident who has paid promptly for at least six months. This waiver will be noted on a chart of outstanding rents and late fees.

Collect as many rents and late fees as required according to your chart of outstanding rents and late fees.

Except for the few days after the cutoff date (tenth of month) established by the asset manager, make bank deposits daily.

Fax a copy of the resident manager's chart of collections to the asset manager each time a rent or late fee is collected and deposited.

1.6   Paperwork

It is **imperative** that all paperwork and documentation be **complete** and **accurate**. Check all work **thoroughly** before submitting it to the asset manager.

If you are unclear about an accounting or paperwork procedure, call the asset manager for clarification. **Do not** submit any work based on an assumption. Incorrect work will be returned to the property for correction.

Generally speaking, the following should be completed for all incoming invoices, deposit slips, chart of collections, etc.:

- Fax a copy to asset manager with Letter of Transmittal.

- Make a copy for the tenant file.

- Make a copy for your records with copy of the Letter of Transmittal.

- Put the original in an interoffice envelope for the asset manager. Keep this envelope in a locked file cabinet until it is retrieved by the asset manager.

1.7   Repairs

The resident manager will keep an updated list of service/repair contractors (the "**team**") that have been approved by the asset manager.

Emergency repairs can be completed immediately by a team member in accordance with the preapproved contract with them:

- Fax a request for service and invoice to the asset manager.

- The asset manager will mail a check to the team member within forty-eight hours.

Normal maintenance can be performed by team members with the asset manager's approval (resolve within seven days or by agreed appointment).

- Itemize on a **request for service** associated costs per item or have a team member provide a quote **statement of repairs required** and fax it to the asset manager for approval.

Resident: The resident is responsible for the first $150 of repairs to the apartment and its appliances due to cause.

- If the resident requests repairs on items due too normal "wear and tear," the resident manager shall comply with resident's request in a timely manner. For normal "wear and tear," there is no charge to the resident.

- The resident manager should collect the $150 premium before commencing with the resident's repairs (cause). If the damage is a safety or health hazard, then the repair must be completed immediately, and the asset manager will bill the resident. In all cases, the resident manager should never argue with the resident, and the repair should be completed in a timely fashion.

- If the resident makes repairs to the apartment, he or she is responsible for it and will not be reimbursed for his or her expended monies.

- The resident manager should **never** make any repairs to the apartment.

1.8   Over Demanding Resident

In spite of careful and thorough background checks, there will always be that difficult resident. For examples is: resident is over demanding and requests continuous and unrealistic amounts of work and effort on your part, such as touch-up painting, fixing leaking toilets, etc.

When dealing with a resident who calls you at all hours wanting immediate attention and repairs, you must be firm and focused:

- Do not jump to respond to every phone call. Assure the resident that you will fix the problem during normal maintenance. Remind the resident of the $150 premium that must be paid up front.

- If the complaint is as simple as securing a loose doorknob, show the resident how to do it.

- If the resident wants improvements not outlined in the lease agreement or policies, he or she will have to secure a contractor to perform the work. Any damages to the apartment will be repaired at the resident's expense.

Note: before commencing with this work, the resident must obtain the asset manager's approval in writing.

If a resident damages the property, he or she is responsible for the cost of repairs. **This is stated in the lease that he or she signed!**

For all work to be done, have the team member come in and provide you with an estimate. Upon receipt, fax a request for service and the estimate to the asset manager, who will then enter the quote into the system. After the asset manager has entered the quote, you will receive a service request via fax. Make two copies:

- The original, stapled to the original estimate, goes to your tenant file.

- Keep a copy for the resident to sign off on.

- Keep a copy for the resident.

Schedule and coordinate work to be performed with the team member and the resident.

If the resident refuses to sign off on the repair, leave him or her with a copy and schedule repair as stated above. Send a copy of the service request that he or she was to sign and write on it the current circumstances. Put this copy in your file. The asset manager will bill him or her according to the lease agreement.

If the resident draws complaints from neighbors about noise and disturbance:

- Advise the resident that his or her neighbors have complained about the noise.

- If you receive a second complaint, have the person complaining call the police about the disturbance.

- If the disturbance continues, fax the complaint to the asset manager and put the original in your file. The asset manager will send the offending tenant a letter warning him or her about breaking the house rules for noise, disturbances, etc. and that all infractions are grounds for eviction.

1.9   Expenses and Materials

Obtain authorization from the asset manager for expenditures in excess of $100.

Maintain petty cash receipts for reimbursement. Provide a copy at the end of the month to the asset manager.

Always order all materials through the asset manager.

Always use approved vendors, since they will bill the asset manager directly.

1.10 Team Members

All team members must file a certificate of insurance with the asset manager showing that they have adequate levels of **liability insurance** and are up to date on their **workmen's compensation insurance**. All capital projects will, in addition to the foregoing, require a **surety bond** protecting the property owner if the contractor does not complete the work.

Team members are contractors licensed in the state to perform the work that their license is issued for. In being licensed, the asset manager is protected in knowing that the contractor has passed state mandated tests, and has specific work experience. Additionally, the asset manager has verified that there are no impending lawsuits or judgements, and that the contractor is professional and reliable, and that all necessary insurance is in place. The list of team members to include:

- Pest control exterminator;

- Locksmith;

- Burglar alarm service;

- Chimney service;

- Appliance repair and service;

- Mold, asbestos, and lead abatement contractor;

- Window replacement technician;

- Drywall contractor;

- Plumbing contractor;

- HVAC contractor;

- Electrical contractor;

- Painting contractor;

- Roofing contractor; and

- Landscape contractor.

Sign all team member invoices after inspecting and approving the work performed. Fax these invoices to the asset manager.

Notify residents of any special projects about to be done in or around the apartment.

Take measures to ensure the safety of your residents and their property all the time but particularly while work is being performed in their apartments and while special projects are in progress. Continually supervise team members. Take action to improve the general appearance of the property, always being alert for any deferred maintenance problems.

1.11 Safety
Verify that locking devices on all exterior doors and windows work.

Keep key logs on all apartment keys and reconcile daily.

The master key must not leave the property. The resident manager and asset manager are the only people with master keys. The resident manager must note in the master key log the day and time the master key was removed, as well as the time and day it was returned.

1.12 Legal

Post three-day notices promptly on the fifth of the month.

Post notices as required. File all copies in the residents' files.

Document each case thoroughly since it may take one year or more for a case to receive a court date.

1.13 Asset Manager

The asset manager is the owner or co-owner of the investment property. In addition to communicating with the resident manager, the asset manager monitors the financial performance (studies the local market, compares individual properties against a norm) of the properties in the investment portfolio. The asset manager supports the resident manager by

- Advertising for residents;

- Organizing and producing rental agreements;

- Renewing leases;

- Managing property;

- Collecting/depositing rents, paying bills, and other accounting tasks;

- Staying informed on landlord laws, policies, rents, and advice;

- Staying informed on fair housing laws and informing the resident manager of same; and

- Maintaining the corporate website.

The asset manager will retain both hard copy and computerized records of all property and resident transactions.

- Hard copy records will be retained for four years.

- Computerized records will be retained for seven years.

The asset manager will formulate and review with the resident manager each year:

- Optimum rents; and

- Operating budget.

1.14 Owner's Equipment

In order to work congruently with the asset manager, the resident manager is loaned the following tools:

- Laptop computer;

- Multifunction printer (with copy, e-mail, network scan, PC fax, and print functions);

- Online Internet and voice services; and

- Cordless phone with digital answering machine.

1.15 Flow Table

The following flow table illustrates how items are catalogued.

File Z	Advertisements, brochures, applications	
	Insurance, license, permits, inspections, service contracts, utilities, floor plans, photographs	
	Keys and key control, resident manager's handbook, TOWS	Resident manager's drawer
	Originals on hold or asset manager to pick up	Asset manager's drawer
File Y	Equipment, appliance warranties	
	Make-ready services	
	Repair and maintenance, preventative maintenance details, and books	
	Capital improvements	
File X	Applications, leases, correspondence, legal, photographs	Current residents
	Applications, Decline Letter	Declined applicants
	Applications, leases, correspondence, legal	Expired residents

Generally speaking, the resident manager gives the applying person an application. Upon completion, the application is faxed to the asset manager for approval or disapproval.

- If the applicant is not approved, the original goes into the asset manager's drawer, and a copy is put in File X— Applications. The asset manager notifies the applicant.

- If the applicant is approved, the lease is e-mailed to the resident manager to obtain signatures. Once the lease is signed, the tenant retains a copy, a copy goes to File Z (asset manager drawer), and a copy goes to the File X—Resident file.

The resident manager keeps all items listed in the various files as indicated. Original copies (equipment, appliance warranties, make-ready services, repair and maintenance, preventative maintenance, and capital improvements) are sent to File Z (asset manager), and copies are distributed as required.

The resident manager should have a copy of the insurance policies, licenses, permits, inspections, service contracts, utilities, floor plans photographs, keys and the key control, and, of course, the resident manager's handbook and TOWS.

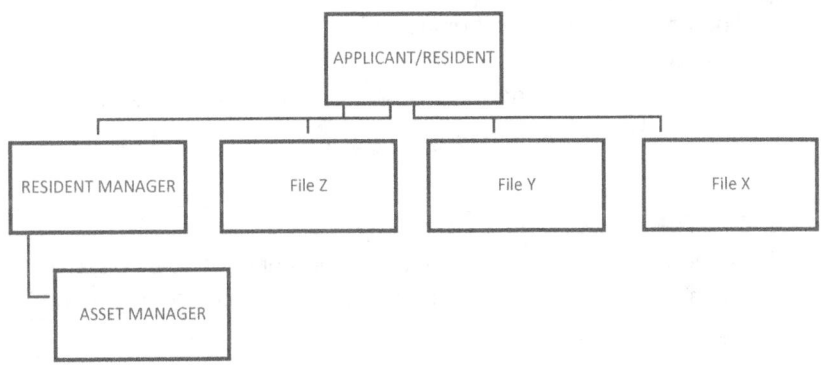

SECTION 2   MAKE READY SERVICES

2.0   General

The resident manager is to be available to monitor the work of others performing the work in this section.

2.1   Make-Ready Painting

We use experienced painters that know what it takes to transform a well-lived-in apartment into the look and detail of a custom home. Report any structural damages to the asset manager.

Before Painting

Remove all outlet covers and switch plates
Sweep baseboards
Spackle all nail holes
Molding and trim, air conditioning grills
Closet and closet rods
Exterior doors, interior doors, outside storage room doors, hallway, living room, kitchen, bathroom

2.2   Make-Ready Cleaning

Skilled housekeepers know the extra efforts needed to clean and refresh an apartment into the look and feel of a brand-new home. Items to be cleaned:

Entrance

Clean front door inside and out

Kitchen

Clean all appliances inside and out
Clean sides, behind, and underneath refrigerator and stove
Clean inside of all drawers, cabinets and pantries
Clean vent hood and replace filter
Replace drip pans on stove as necessary
Replace ice trays with two new trays, and leave in plastic sales cover
Clean and oil cabinets

Clean and polish sinks, faucets, and countertops
Replace faucet washers
Clean faucet aerator and flow restrictor
Replace refrigerator light
Replace lightbulbs

Bathroom
Clean and polish sink, tub, and toilet
Clean and polish faucet, spout, and shower diverter
Replace faucet washers
Clean faucet aerator and flow restrictor
Clean shower head flow restrictor
Clean and polish tiles
Clean and polish countertop and mirrors
Clean inside of all drawers and cabinets
Clean and polish all light fixtures and vents
Replace lightbulbs

Miscellaneous
Sweep, mop, and polish all floors
Vacuum all carpeting
Shampoo carpeting
Clean closet shelves and rods
Clean windows inside and out
Clean light fixtures
Replace all switch plates and outlet covers with new ones
Clean air conditioning vents
Clean outside porch light fixture and replace bulb
Sweep porch, patio/balcony, and storage areas
Clean ceiling fans and replace all bulbs
Clean fireplace

2.3   Make-Ready Maintenance
Team maintenance technicians ensure that everything is in perfect
working condition.

General
Doors (threshold, weather strip, door stop, doorbell, keys)
vent hood

Cabinet doors (knobs, hinges, friction catches)
Kitchen countertops
Kitchen floor
Kitchen sink (faucets, O-rings, seats, washers, aerators, trap, drain)
Disposal
Dishwasher
Stove (burners)
Oven (element, broiler pan)
Refrigerator (crisper, glass, meat tray, door seal, ice trays)
Bathroom floor
Water closet (ball cock, flush, bowl, seat)
Lavatory (trap, drain, pop-up, O-ring, seat, washer)
Tissue holder
Towel racks
Bathtub (stopper, popup, tile, grout, valves, O-ring, seat, washer,
Shower head, soap dish)
Bathroom cabinets (door, drawer)
Air conditioning (filter, knob, cooling)
Heat
Windows (locks, screens)
Mini-blinds/drapes (rod, cord)
Outlets
Switches
Molding and trim
Wall covering
Sheetrock, walls, ceiling
Fireplace
Remove old caulk and recaulk as needed.

Final
Door locks
Keyless bolting device
Sliding door lock, latch
Window locks
Smoke detectors (replace battery)
Intrusion alarm
Fire extinguisher (check dates)

2.4   Available Services

There are times when a tenant may want to have his or her apartment spruced up. Pricing for available services:

Service	Studio	1 BR	2BR	3BR
Painting	$325	$450	$600	$750
Cleaning	$185	$195	$215	$225
Maintenance	$75	$85	$95	$125
Subtotal	$585	$730	$910	$1,080
Discount	-$40	-$50	-$50	-$80
Final cost	**$545**	**$680**	**$860**	**$1,000**

SECTION 3   RESIDENT'S REPAIRS

3.0   Resident-Responsible Repairs

As the asset manager, you accept responsibility for nearly all of the maintenance to the structure and exterior of the property. However, there is a range of repair items that remain the responsibility of the resident to maintain.

The following is a list of repairs the resident is expected to maintain:

- replacement of front and back door locks when keys have been lost or stolen (This includes getting into the property and repairing any damage to the door or lock. A complete set must be given to the resident manager.)

- getting additional keys cut;

- supply and fitting of additional security items such as extra locks, door chains, peepholes, security alarms, etc. (unless part of an agreed security upgrade);

- repair/replacement of curtain rails;

- supplying and fitting window blinds;

- arranging for washing machines to be plumbed in;

- internal decorating of property and repair of minor plaster cracks;

- arranging for telephone/media connection points to be installed and maintained;

- repairing items damaged by abuse or neglect;

- supplying and fitting clothes dryers and line posts;

- repairs to do it yourself work;

- unblocking sink and drainage pipes caused by inappropriate waste; and

- purchasing of tenant insurance to ensure that you are covered for any damage arising from leaks, burst pipes, etc.

APPENDIX A

.

Description of Work

by

Property Type

Level 1	Single Family: Town House; Condo
Level 2	Low Rise
Level 3	Mid Rise
Level 4	High Rise

See schedule below for location and level of service.

A. Outside
Level 1
Pick up papers and other litter on the grounds and sidewalks. Look at the property's exterior, noting the condition of eaves and trim, roof, porches, parking areas, fire escapes, and any other common areas, scrutinizing them for defects that require immediate attention and capital outlay. The resident manager is responsible for taking the trash containers to the designated curbside for pickup and then taking the emptied containers back to their designated resting spot. Keep this area clean and free from debris at all times. During the winter months, shovel snow from the walkways.

Levels 2, 3, and 4
If there is an on-site container from which the trash service removes the trash, then the area must be kept free from debris at all times.

Levels 1 and 2 (weekly)
Mow lawn and rake leaves as required.

Levels 1 and 2 (monthly)
Trim bushes and trees and fertilize lawn and plants.

Levels 1 and 2 (every six months)
Inspect roof and clean gutters.

B. Inside

Levels 1 to 4
Generally, tour the building's entranceways, halls, basement, laundry room, boiler room, and other interior common interior areas to check for routine upkeep of machinery, equipment, and amenities, noting their condition and performance. Report to the asset manager any equipment that appears not to be working to specifications and all health and safety hazards.

Levels 1 to 4
Weekly: Clean stairway and foyers, clean laundry facilities and collect money, and replace burnt-out lightbulbs.

Monthly: Clean basement area.

Quarterly: Inspect common areas for damage and wear and tear (report findings to asset manager), and change filters in furnace and air conditioners.

Every six months: Change batteries in smoke detectors, carbon monoxide detectors, and radon detectors in common areas; change batteries in residents' carbon monoxide/smoke detectors; clean windows in common areas; and have carpets in hallways and stairs professionally cleaned.

Annual tasks: Have furnace, water heater, and air conditioning serviced by team member.

C. Outside

Same as for level 1 above.

D. Inside

Meet all of the requirements as listed for level 1 above, and handle all general repairs and maintenance for the residential units. Notify the asset manager of all items that need replacement, repair, or painting. Make ready all vacated units so that they may be re-rented as soon as possible.

APPENDIX B

NONDISCLOSURE AGREEMENT

THIS NONDISCLOSURE AGREEMENT (the "Agreement") is entered into by and between the Asset Manager with its principal offices at
_____ ("Disclosing Party")
and _____ located at_____
_____ ("Receiving Party") for the purposes of preventing the unauthorized disclosure of Confidential Information as defined below. The parties agree to enter into a confidential relationship with respect to the disclosure of certain propriety and confidential information ("Confidential Information").

1. **Definition of Confidential Information**. For purposes of this Agreement, "**Confidential Information**" shall include all information or material that has or could have commercial value or other utility in the business in which Disclosing Party is engaged. If Confidential Information is in written form, the Disclosing Party shall label or stamp the materials with the word "Confidential" or some similar warning. If Confidential Information is transmitted orally, the Disclosing Party shall promptly follow up in writing, to the recipient that such oral communication constitutes Confidential Information.

2. **Exclusions from Confidential Information**. Receiving Party's obligations under this Agreement do not extend to information that is (a) publicly known at the time of disclosure or subsequently becomes publicly known through no fault of the Receiving Party, (b) discovered or created by the Receiving Party before disclosure by Disclosing Party, (c) learned by the Receiving Party through legitimate means other than from the Disclosing Party or Disclosing Party's representatives, or (d) disclosed by Receiving Party with Disclosing Party's prior written approval.

3. **Obligations of Receiving Party**. Receiving Party shall hold and maintain the Confidential Information in strictest confidence for the sole and exclusive benefit of the Disclosing Party. Receiving Party shall carefully restrict access to Confidential Information to employees, contractors, and third parties as is reasonably required and shall require those persons to sign nondisclosure restrictions at least as protective as those in this Agreement. Receiving Party shall not, without prior written approval of Disclosing Party, use for Receiving Party's own benefit, publish, copy, or otherwise disclose to others, or permit the use by others for their benefit or

29

to the detriment of Disclosing Party, any Confidential Information. Receiving Party shall return to Disclosing Party any and all records, notes, and other written, printed, or tangible materials in its possession pertaining to Confidential Information immediately if Disclosing Party requests it in writing.

4. **Time Periods**. The nondisclosure provisions of this Agreement shall survive the termination of this Agreement and Receiving Party's duty to hold Confidential Information in confidence shall remain in effect until the Confidential Information no longer qualifies as a trade secret or until Disclosing Party sends Receiving Party written notice releasing Receiving Party from this Agreement, whichever occurs first.

5. **Relationships**. Nothing contained in this Agreement shall be deemed to constitute either party a partner, joint venture, or employee of the other party for any purpose.

6. **Severability**. If a court finds any provision of this Agreement invalid or unenforceable, the remainder of this Agreement shall be interpreted so as best to affect the intent of the parties.

7. **Integration**. This Agreement expresses the complete understanding of the parties with respect to the subject matter and supersedes all prior proposals, agreements, representations, and understandings. This Agreement may not be amended except in writing signed by both parties.

8. **Waiver**. The failure to exercise any right provided in this Agreement shall not be a waiver of prior or subsequent rights.

This Agreement and each party's obligations shall be binding on the representatives, assigns, and successors of such party. Each party has signed this Agreement through its authorized representative.

By:_____   By:_____

Title: _____   Title: _____

Date: _____   Date: _____

       Resident Manager   Asset Manager

APPENDIX C

INDEPENDENT CONTRACTOR AGREEMENT

FOR

RESIDENT MANAGER

SAMPLE DOCUMENT

INDEPENDENT CONTRACTOR AGREEMENT

FOR

RESIDENT MANAGER

THIS INDEPENDENT CONTRACTOR'S AGREEMENT (the "Agreement") is made as of 20__ by and between (the Company) and
_____ (the Independent Contractor), a sole proprietorship with its principal place of business at
_____.

In consideration of the mutual premises herein contained, Company and Independent Contractor hereby agree as follows:

SECTION 1: ENGAGEMENT

The Company hereby engages the Independent Contractor to render the services according to the schedule and as described in the annexed Exhibit A (collectively, the "Services"). We cannot accept for management any person that does not comply with **Fair Housing Laws**.

In the event of any conflict between this Agreement and the annexed Exhibit A, this Agreement shall control.

SECTION 2: SCHEDULE OF SERVICES TO BE PERFORMED BY INDEPENDENT CONTRACTOR

The Independent Contractor agrees to show apartments, provide applications, and collect application fees; to be responsible for the inventory of tools, supplies, furniture, and master keys of the complex; and to communicate with the residents and handle day-to-day issues.

The Independent Contractor agrees to collect late rents and other added rent as they become due and as directed by the Asset Manager. The Independent Contractor is to render to the Asset Manager a monthly accounting of rents and added rents received and deposited and expenses paid.

Independent Contractor agrees to supervise all employees, vendors, team members, and other needed labor.

SECTION 3: COMPENSATION

A. In full consideration for the performance of the Services hereunder and for any rights granted or relinquished by the Independent Contractors under this Agreement, the Company shall pay the Independent Contractor as follows (check as applicable):

---- A fixed fee (the "Fee") in the amount of $ payable in monthly installments for as long as this agreement is in effect.

---- Rent credit in the amount of $_____ payable in monthly installments for as long as this agreement is in effect.

---- Cable telephone/Internet service credit in the amount of $_____ payable in monthly installments for as long as this agreement is in effect.

B. Payments shall be preceded by an invoice from the Independent Contractor (to be submitted monthly), which Company shall then pay in the ordinary course of business.

C. The Company will reimburse the Independent Contractor reasonable and necessary expenses incurred in the performance of the Services provided, however, that all such expenses shall be subject to the Company's prior approval.

D. Independent Contractor acknowledges and agrees that, except as provided in Section 3, it shall not be entitled to and the Company shall not be obligated to pay any monies or other compensation for the Services provided and rights granted under this Agreement.

SECTION 4: ASSURANCE OF SERVICES

A. Independent Contractor will assure that the following individuals (the "Key Employees") will be available to perform and will perform the Services hereunder until they are completed:

Name of Key Employee: _____

Name of Key Employee: _____

The Key Employees may be changed only with the prior written approval of the Company; which approval shall not be unreasonably withheld. If none, enter "**NONE**."

SECTION 5: INDEPENDENT CONTRACTOR RELATIONSHIP

A. The Independent Contractor agrees to perform the Services hereunder solely as an Independent Contractor. The parties to this Agreement recognize that this Agreement does not create any actual or apparent agency, partnership, franchise, or relationship of employer and employee between the parties. The Independent Contractor is not authorized to enter into or commit the Company to any agreements, and the Independent Contractor shall not represent itself as the agent or legal representative of the Company.

B. Further, the Independent Contractor shall not be entitled to participate in any of the Company's benefits, including without limitation any health or retirement plans. The Independent Contractor shall not be entitled to any remuneration, benefits, or expenses other than as specifically provided for in this Agreement.

C. The Company shall not be liable for taxes, workmen's compensation insurance, unemployment insurance, employer's liability, employer's FICA, Social Security, withholding tax, or other taxes or withholding for or on behalf of the Independent Contractor in performing Services under this Agreement. All such costs shall be Independent Contractor's responsibility.

SECTION 6: PROPRIETARY RIGHTS

A. The Independent Contractor acknowledges that it has no right to or interest in its work or product resulting from the Services performed hereunder, or created by the Independent Contractor in connection with such Services. The Independent Contractor acknowledges that the Services and the products thereof (hereinafter referred to as the "Materials") have been specially commissioned or ordered by the Company as "works made-for-hire" as that term is used in the Copyright Law of the United States, and that the Company is therefore to be deemed the author of and is the owner of all copyrights in and to such Material.

B. In the event that such Materials, or any portion thereof, are for any reason deemed not to have been works made-for-hire, the Independent Contractor hereby assigns to the Company any and all rights, title, and interest Independent Contractor may have in and to such Materials, including all copyrights, all publishing rights, and all rights to use, reproduce, and otherwise exploit the Materials in any and all formats or media and all channels, whether now known or hereafter created. The Independent Contractor agrees to execute such instruments as the Company may from time to time deem necessary or desirable to evidence, establish, maintain, and protect the Company's ownership of such Materials, and all other rights, title, and interest therein.

SECTION 7: CONFIDENTIALITY

A. In connection with the performance of Services hereunder, the Independent Contractor may be exposed to confidential and proprietary information of the Company, whether or not so identified (including without limitations this Agreement). All such confidential and proprietary information shall be subject to the terms and conditions of the Nondisclosure Agreement, as annexed in Exhibit B.

B. The Independent Contractor shall not, without the prior written consent of the Company, use the Company's name in any advertising or promotional literature or publish any articles relating to the Company, this Agreement, or the Services provided.

SECTION 8: WARRANTIES AND INDEMNIFICATION

A. The Independent Contractor represents and warrants:

   a. The Services shall be performed in accordance with and shall not violate applicable laws, rules or regulations, and standards prevailing in the industry and the Independent Contractor shall obtain all permits or permissions required to comply with such laws, rules, or regulations.

b.   The Materials shall be original, clear, and presentable in accordance with generally applicable standards in the industry.

c.   The Materials will not contain libelous, injurious, or unlawful materials and will not violate or in any way infringe upon the personal or propriety rights of third parties, including property, contractual, employment, trade secrets, propriety information, and nondisclosure rights, or any trademark, copyright, or patent, nor will they contain any format, instruction, or information that is inaccurate or injurious to any person, computer system, or machine.

d.   The Independent Contractor has full power and authority to enter into and perform its obligations under this Agreement. This Agreement is a legal, valid, and binding obligation of the Independent Contractor, enforceable against it in accordance with its terms (except as may be limited by bankruptcy, insolvency, moratorium, or similar laws affecting creditors' rights generally and equitable remedies). Entering into this Agreement will not violate the Charter or Bylaws of the Independent Contractor or any material contract to which it is a party.

e.   The Independent Contractor will perform the Services in accordance with the specifications established by the Company.

B.   The Company represents and warrants that it has full power and authority to enter into and perform its obligations under this Agreement; this Agreement is a legal, valid, and binding obligation of the Company, enforceable against it in accordance with its terms (except as may be limited by bankruptcy, insolvency, moratorium, or similar laws affecting creditors' rights generally and equitable remedies); entering into this Agreement will not violate the Charter or Bylaws of the Company or any material contract to which it is a party.

C.   The Independent Contractor shall comply with all of the Company's standards and procedures when working on site at the Company, including, without limitation, standards relating to security.

D.   The Company shall not be liable for injury or death occurring to the Independent Contractor or any of its employees or other assistants in the course of performing services stated in this Agreement.

E.   The Independent Contractor hereby indemnifies and holds harmless the Company, its subsidiaries, and affiliates, and their officers and employees, from any damages, claims, liabilities, and costs, including reasonable attorney's fees, or losses of any kind or nature whatsoever the "Loss" which may in any way arise from the Services performed by the Independent Contractor hereunder, or any breach or alleged breach by the Independent Contractor of this Agreement, including the warranties set forth herein. The Company shall retain control over the defense of, and any resolution or settlement relating to, such Loss. The Independent Contractor will cooperate with the Company and provide reasonable assistance in defending any such claim.

SECTION 9: TERM AND TERMINATION

A.   The term of this Agreement shall commence on the date hereof and shall continue until the Independent Contractor satisfactorily completes performance of the Services (hereinafter the "Term").

B.   This Agreement may be terminated:

   a.   By either party upon thirty (30) days' prior written notice if the other party breaches or is in default of any obligation hereunder and such default has not been cured within such thirty-day period.

   b.   By the Company at any time during the Term for any reason (or no reason) upon ten (10) days' written notice.

C.   Neither party shall be liable or deemed to be in default for any delay or failure in performance under this Agreement or interruption of service resulting, directly or indirectly, from acts of God, civil or military authority, acts of the public enemy, war, riots, civil disturbances, insurrections, accidents, fire, explosions, earthquakes, floods, the elements, strikes, labor disputes, shortages of suitable parts, materials, labor, transportation, or any causes beyond the control of such party.

D.   Upon termination by either party, Independent Contractor shall provide to Company any and all copies, in whole or in part, of the Materials (as they then exist), all equipment loaned to Independent Contractor, and any and all tangible materials the Company provided to the Independent Contractor in connection with this Agreement.

SECTION 10: DAMAGES AND REMEDIES

A.   In the event of termination of this Agreement by the Company pursuant to Section 8.B, the Company shall have all remedies available to it by law.

B. In the event of termination pursuant to Section 8.B, and provided that Independent Contractor is not in material breach of its obligations hereunder, the Independent Contractor shall be entitled to keep all monies already paid pursuant to Section 3, and the Company's sole obligation shall be to pay Independent Contractor the amount due for Services already acceptably performed and Materials already accepted, pro rata. In no event shall the Company be liable for any lost profits or consequential, incidental, or special damage.

C. The Independent Contractor waives any and all right to injunctive relief in the event of any dispute with the Company, and the Independent Contractor's sole remedy in such a dispute shall be at law.

SECTION 11: GENERAL TERMS

A. This Agreement shall be governed and construed in accordance with the laws of the State of _____ applicable to contracts made and fully performed therein, and the state and federal courts located in _____ state shall have exclusive jurisdiction of all suits and proceedings arising out of or in connection with this agreement. Both parties hereby submit to the jurisdiction of said courts for the purposes of any such suit or proceeding and waive any claim that any such forum is an inconvenient forum.

B. Any notices to either party under this Agreement shall be in writing and delivered by hand or sent by nationally recognized messenger service or by registered or certified mail, return receipt requested, to the address set forth above or to such other address as that party may hereafter designate by notice. Notice shall be effective when received, which shall be no greater than one (1) business day after being sent by a nationally recognized messenger service or three days after being sent by mail.

C. The Company may freely assign this Agreement, in whole or in part. The Independent Contractor may not, without the written consent of the Company, assign, subcontract, or delegate its obligations under this Agreement, except that the Independent Contractor may transfer the right only to receive any amounts which may be payable to it for performance under this Agreement, and then only after receipt by the Company of written notice of such assignment or transfer. This Agreement shall be binding upon and inure to the benefit of the parties' successors and assigns.

D. The waiver by either party of a breach or violation of any provision of this Agreement shall not constitute a waiver of any subsequent or other breach or violation.

E. Following the expiration or termination of this Agreement, whether by its terms, operation of law, or otherwise, the terms and conditions set forth, as well as any term, provision, or condition required for the interpretation of this Agreement or necessary for the full observation and performance by each party hereto of all rights and obligations arising prior to the date of termination, shall survive such expiration or termination.

F. This Agreement represents the entire Agreement between the parties. The Agreement may not be amended, changed, or supplemented in any way except by written Agreement signed by both parties.

This is a legal document. The Independent Contractor is aware that he or she has the right to obtain legal counsel prior to the execution of this agreement.

By: _____

Title: _____

Date: _____

Residential Manager

By: _____

Title: _____

Date: _____

Asset Manager

APPENDIX D

FAIR HOUSING

REFERENCE

RESIDENT MANAGER

We are providing the following information so that the resident manager will have a basic understanding of the Fair Housing Act. It is company policy to abide by said laws and to comply with all state[1] and local laws pertaining to same.

These laws specifically prohibit discrimination. You may not

- deny a dwelling

- refuse to rent

- make housing unavailable

- set different terms, conditions or privileges for rental

- provide different housing services or facilities

- falsely deny that housing is available for rent

to anyone because of their race, color, national origin, religion, sex, disability and the presence of children.

Additionally, it is illegal to

- threaten, coerce, intimidate or interfere with anyone exercising a fair housing right or assisting others who exercise that right

- advertise or make any statement that indicates a limitation or preference based on race, color, national origin, religion, sex, familial status, or handicap.

---

[1] http://www.civilrights.org/fairhousing/laws/state-laws.html

Fair Housing Laws

The following has been copied from the HUD website so that the resident manager can read and obtain a further understanding of federal law regarding the sections copied.

Fair Housing Act
Title VIII of the Civil Rights Act of 1968 (Fair Housing Act), as amended, prohibits discrimination in the sale, rental, and financing of dwellings, and in other housing-related transactions, based on race, color, national origin, religion, sex, familial status (including children under the age of 18 living with parents or legal custodians, pregnant women, and people securing custody of children under the age of 18), and disability.

Title VI of the Civil Rights Act of 1964
Title VI prohibits discrimination on the basis of race, color, or national origin in programs and activities receiving federal financial assistance.

Section 504 of the Rehabilitation Act of 1973
Section 504 prohibits discrimination based on disability in any program or activity receiving federal financial assistance.

Section 109 of Title I of the Housing and Community Development Act of 1974
Section 109 prohibits discrimination on the basis of race, color, national origin, sex or religion in programs and activities receiving financial assistance from HUD's Community Development and Block Grant Program.

Title II of the Americans with Disabilities Act of 1990
Title II prohibits discrimination based on disability in programs, services, and activities provided or made available by public entities. HUD enforces Title II when it relates to state and local public housing, housing assistance and housing referrals.

Architectural Barriers Act of 1968
The Architectural Barriers Act requires that buildings and facilities designed, constructed, altered, or leased with certain federal funds after September 1969 must be accessible to and useable by handicapped persons.

Age Discrimination Act of 1975
The Age Discrimination Act prohibits discrimination on the basis of age in programs or activities receiving federal financial assistance.

Title IX of the Education Amendments Act of 1972
Title IX prohibits discrimination on the basis of sex in education programs or activities that receive federal financial assistance.

Fair Housing-Related Presidential Executive Orders:

Executive Order 11063
Executive Order 11063 prohibits discrimination in the sale, leasing, rental, or other disposition of properties and facilities owned or operated by the federal government or provided with federal funds.

Executive Order 11246
Executive Order 11246, as amended, bars discrimination in federal employment because of race, color, religion, sex, or national origin.

Executive Order 12892
Executive Order 12892, as amended, requires federal agencies to affirmatively further fair housing in their programs and activities, and provides that the Secretary of HUD will be responsible for coordinating the effort. The Order also establishes the President's Fair Housing Council, which will be chaired by the Secretary of HUD.

Executive Order 12898
Executive Order 12898 requires that each federal agency conduct its program, policies, and activities that substantially affect human health or the environment in a manner that does not exclude persons based on race, color, or national origin.

Executive Order 13166
Executive Order 13166 eliminates, to the extent possible, limited English proficiency as a barrier to full and meaningful participation by beneficiaries in all federally-assisted and federally conducted programs and activities.

Executive Order 13217
Executive Order 13217 requires federal agencies to evaluate their policies and programs to determine if any can be revised or modified to improve the availability of community-based living arrangements for persons with disabilities.

For additional information on the above go to
http://portal.hud.gov/hudportal/HUD?src=/program_offices/fair_housing_equal_opp/FHLaws

The Resident Manager's Handbook

www.ingramcontent.com/pod-product-compliance
Lightning Source LLC
Chambersburg PA
CBHW071828200526
45169CB00018B/1197